P9-CED-392

The
Natural Superiority
of
THE
LEFT-HANDER

The Natural Superiority of THE LEFT-HANDER

By James T. de Kay

M. Evans and Company, Inc. New York

The Natural Superiority of THE LEFT-HANDER

By James T. de Kay

M. Evans and Company, Inc.   New York

Library of Congress Cataloging in Publication Data

de Kay, James T
    The natural superiority of the left-hander.

    1. Left- and right-handedness—Caricatures and
cartoons. 2. American wit and humor, Pictorial.
I. Title.
NC1429.D347A4 1979   741.5'973   79-15824
ISBN 0-87131-307-3

Copyright © 1979 by James T. de Kay

All rights reserved. No part of this book may be reproduced
or transmitted in any form or by any means without the written
permission of the publisher.

M. Evans and Company, Inc.
216 East 49 Street
New York, New York 10017

Manufactured in the United States of America

39 38 37 36 35 34 33 32

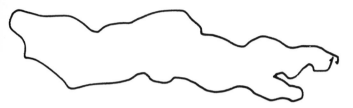

DEDICATED
to the citizens of
LEFT HAND, WEST VIRGINIA

Population 450,
and every one a
Left Hander.

One person in ten is a left-hander. And every last one of them thinks he's sort of special.

Which is probably true . . .

No kidding.
Anywhere you look,
left-handedness is
something of a rarity.

Even most plants
are right-handed.
Honeysuckle is one of
the few climbing plants
that twines to the left.

Most flatfish lie down on
their left side. This makes
them right-handed.

The Pacific sand dab is one of the
few that lies down on the other
side. This makes it left-handed.
Or rather, left-finned.

There are even a few sea
shells that curve left-handedly.
They are prized by collectors.

Lobsters are
sometimes
left-han

ded.

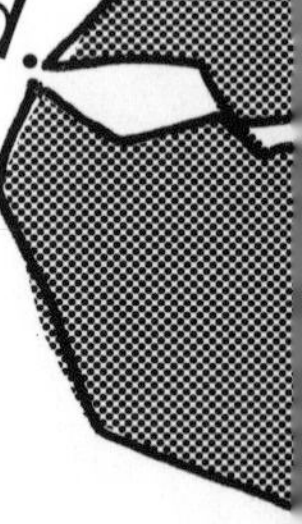

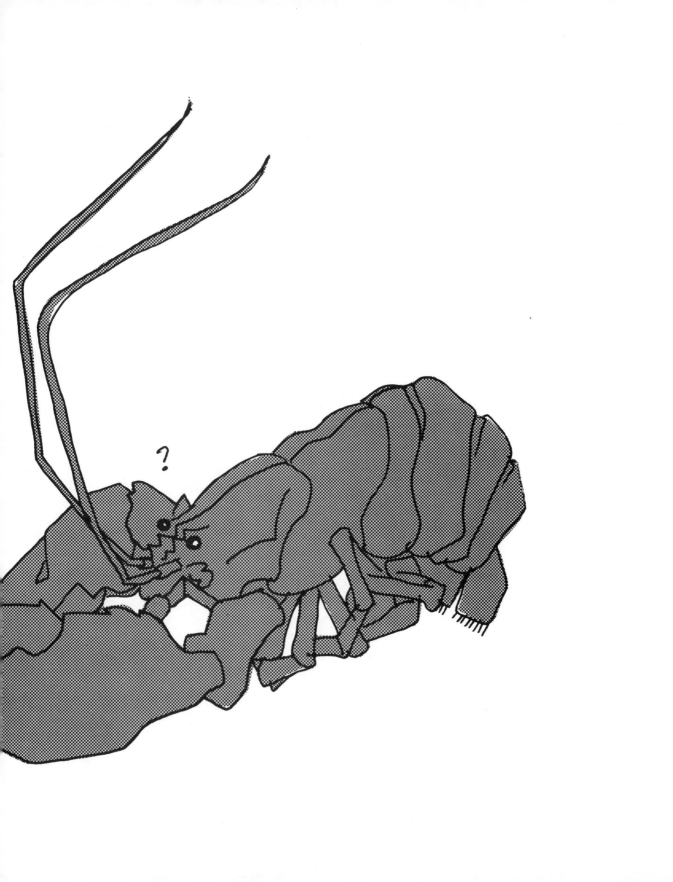

It could be that the
only case where
left-handers are in the
majority is among
gorillas. Their
left arms outweigh their
right, which may
indicate a slight
left-handed bias.
But that's only
speculation.

As far as humans are concerned,
there's evidence that the

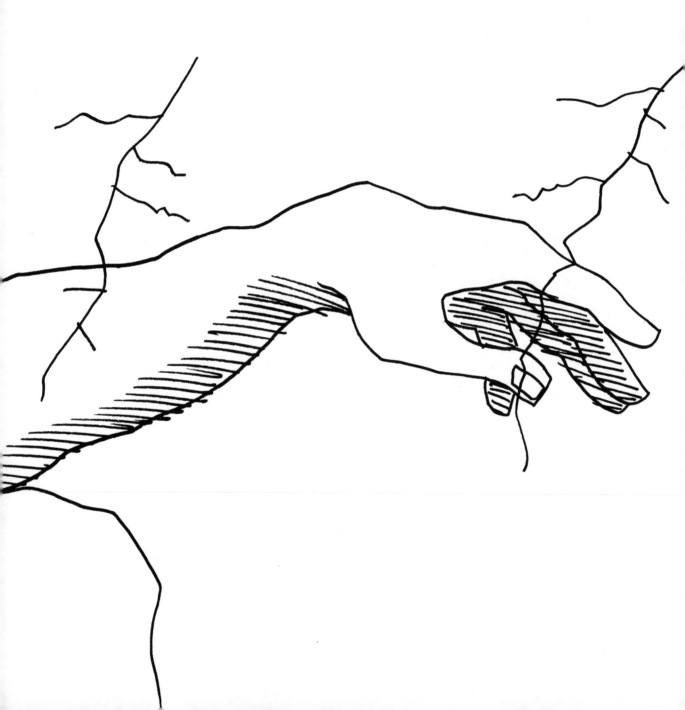

very first member of the
species was left-handed.

In the early days,
as we know from cave drawings,

There were plenty of
right-handers,
but there were plenty of
left-handers, too.

Things were fine for left-handers up through the Stone Age.

But with the Bronze Age came manufacturing. And since most people were right-handed, that's the way they made the tools. To this day, no one has ever made a left-handed sickle.

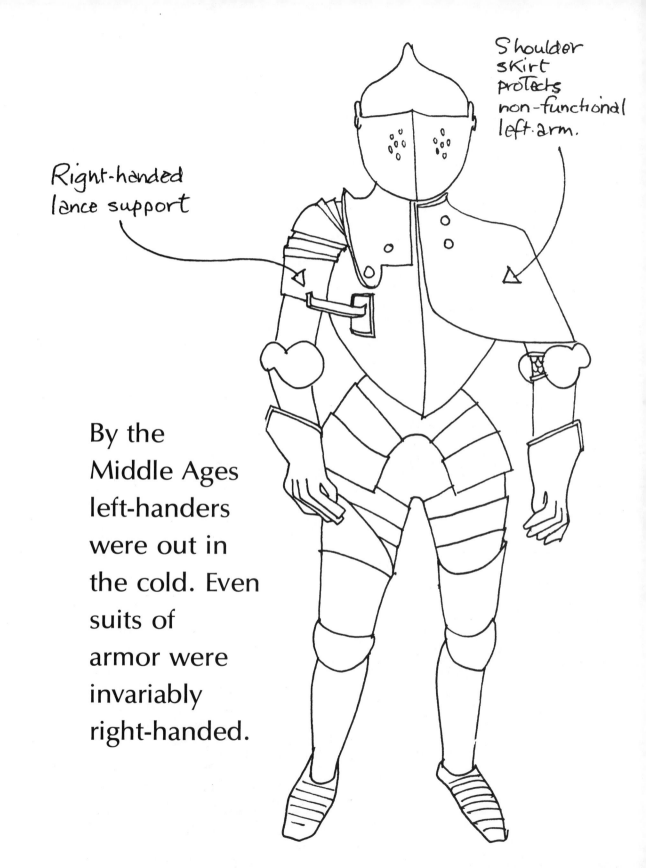

Right-handed
lance support

Shoulder
skirt
protects
non-functional
left arm.

By the
Middle Ages
left-handers
were out in
the cold. Even
suits of
armor were
invariably
right-handed.

That long-ago bias against left-handers is still with us. Bus coin boxes are right-handed.

And so are phonograph tone arms.

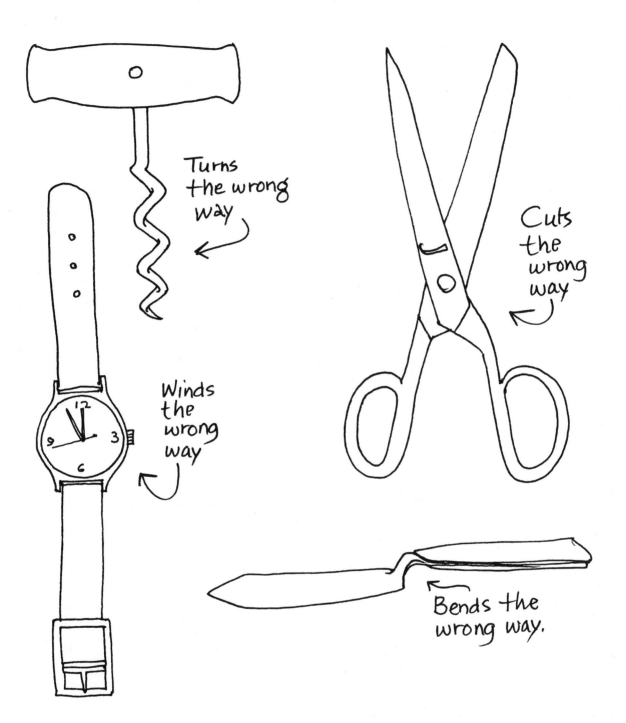

Turns the wrong way

Winds the wrong way

Cuts the wrong way

Bends the wrong way.

It's enough to make left-handers a little paranoid.

Even
carousels are
right-handed.

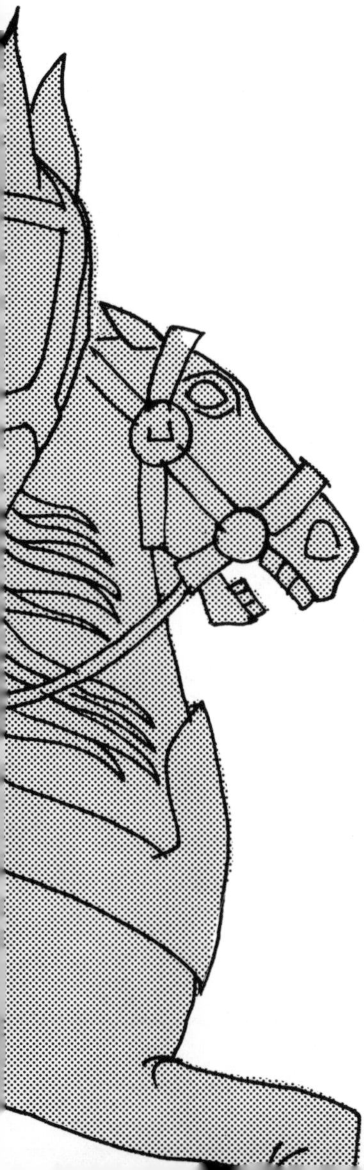

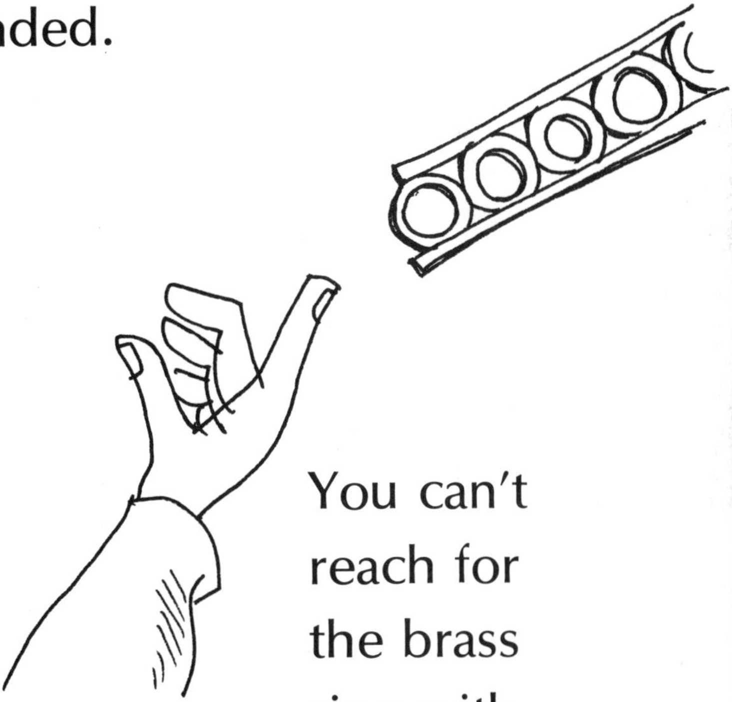

You can't
reach for
the brass
ring with
your left hand.

Today, about the
only thing that
actually favors
left-handers
is the
toll booth.

Of course, if you are a
rich or important
left-hander, you can ignore
all the prejudice.

For instance, it never
bothered Ramses II, who
is always shown as
left-handed.

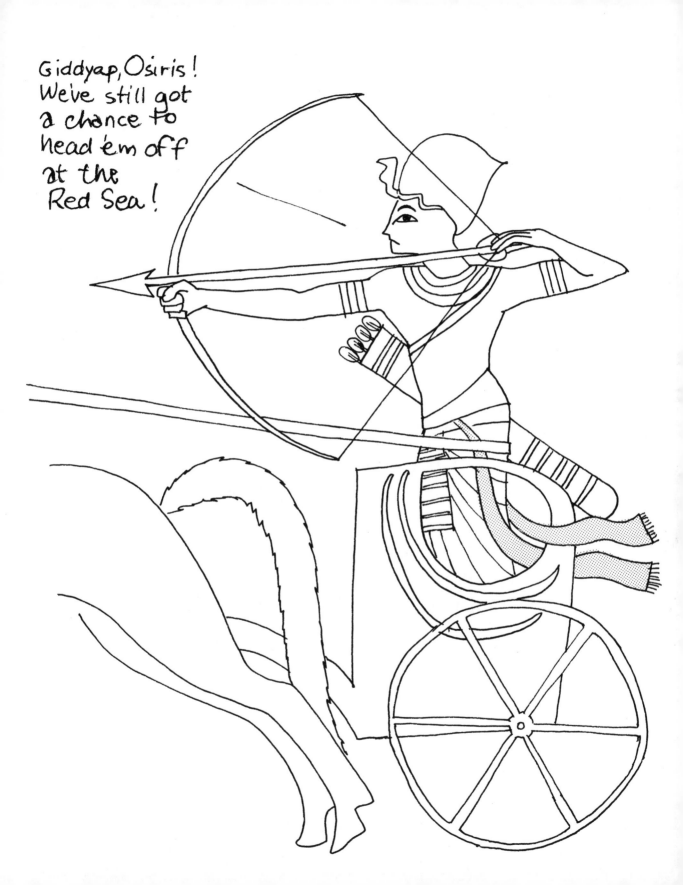

And Ben Franklin
actually gloried in
his left-handedness.
He wrote and published
a treatise in
favor of the
left hand.

JAMES GARFIELD

HARRY TRUMAN

GERALD FORD

There have been three
left-handed Presidents.

NELSON ROCKEFELLER

And one of them
even had a left-handed
Vice-President.

Gerald Ford, by the way,
may be unique. He is
left-handed only when
sitting down.
He throws a ball, plays golf,
and writes on a blackboard
right-handed.

Jimi Hendrix was neither
rich nor important,
but he became
both by beating
right-handers at their
own game. He restrung
his guitar so he
could play it
left-handed.

In sports, there is often an advantage in left-handedness.

This is particularly true in baseball, which may explain why right-handed players are often ambivalent about left-handers.

In golf, left-handed
Ben Hogan played
right-handed because
he was told the greater
strength in his leading
arm would improve his
stroke.

Years later, he
regretted switching.

Swimming also
favors left-handers.
Neurologists have
shown they adjust
more readily to
underwater vision.
Mark Spitz,
who won
seven Olympic gold
medals, is, as you might
expect, left-handed.

But polo is another story.
It's actually
against the rules to play
left-handed.

And that even goes for
the left-handed
Prince of Wales.

For some reason not quite clear, left-handers make fantastic tennis players. At any given time, about 40% of the top pros are left-handed . . . people like Rod Laver, Jimmy Connors, Manuel Orantes, Guillermo Villas, Martina Navratilova, etc.

Sporting footnote:
In 1890, the baseball
diamond in Chicago was
sited to protect the batters
from the late afternoon
sun. In consequence,
the pitcher faced west,
and if he was left-handed,
he was known as a
southpaw.

Where does
left-handedness
come from?
Is it inherited?
Maybe.

But... can something as rigorously right-handed as the DNA helix actually transmit left-handedness?

We know that if both
parents are left-handed,
50% of the kids will be
left-handed too.

But if both parents are
right-handed, only 2% of
the kids will be left-handed.

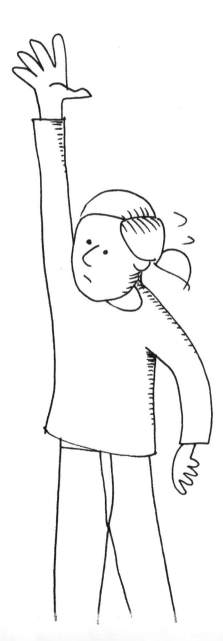

Another indication that
left-handedness is genetic
comes from Scotland's
Kerr family.

For centuries the Kerrs have
been famous for the large number
of left-handers they produce.

They even gave their
castles left-
handed
staircases so they'd be
easy to defend.

At one time,
American Indians
may have been the
world's largest single
population of
left-handers. There's
evidence that
one in three
was left-handed.

The Incas thought
left-handedness was
lucky. One of their
great chiefs was
LLOQUE YUPANQUI,
which means
left-handed.

Inca-dinka-doo.

There's a high incidence of
left-handedness in twins, but it's
rare to find both left-handed.

There are more
left-handed boys than girls.
No one knows why.

Older mothers are more
likely to produce left-handed
children
than younger
mothers.

Some experts claim
they can spot a
left-hander in infancy.
The whorl of their
hair, it is said, will
twist counterclockwise.

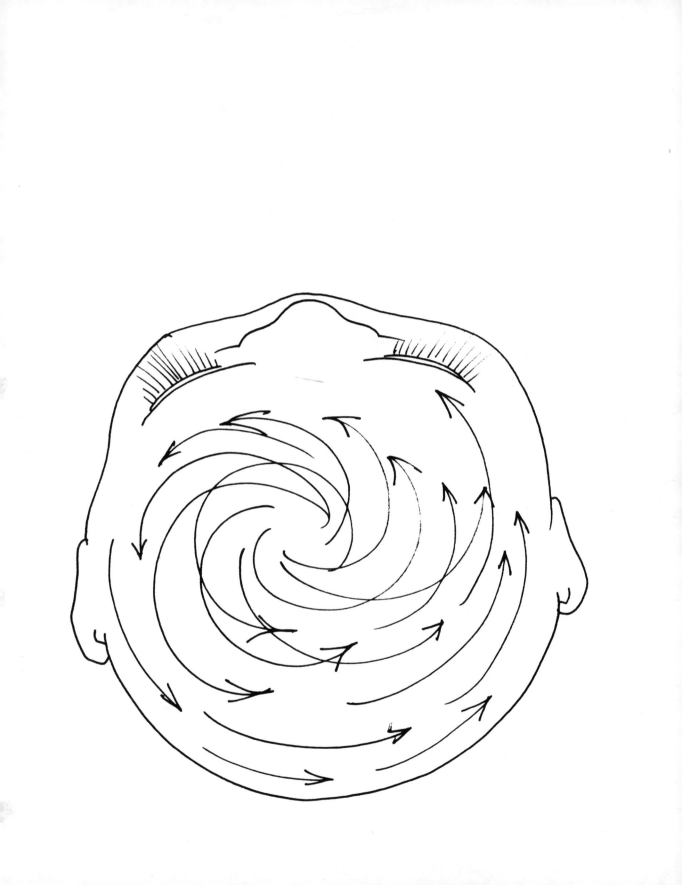

Virtually all
pediatricians will
agree that if a
child has a preference
for the left hand,
it will show up
by age five.

The New England Journal of Medicine suggests you can tell if you're left-handed if the base of your left thumbnail is wider and squarer than the right.

Another researcher,
Theodore Blau, has a
different test. Using
each hand in turn,
draw X's, then circle
them. If you draw the
circles counterclockwise
you're left-handed
(he says).

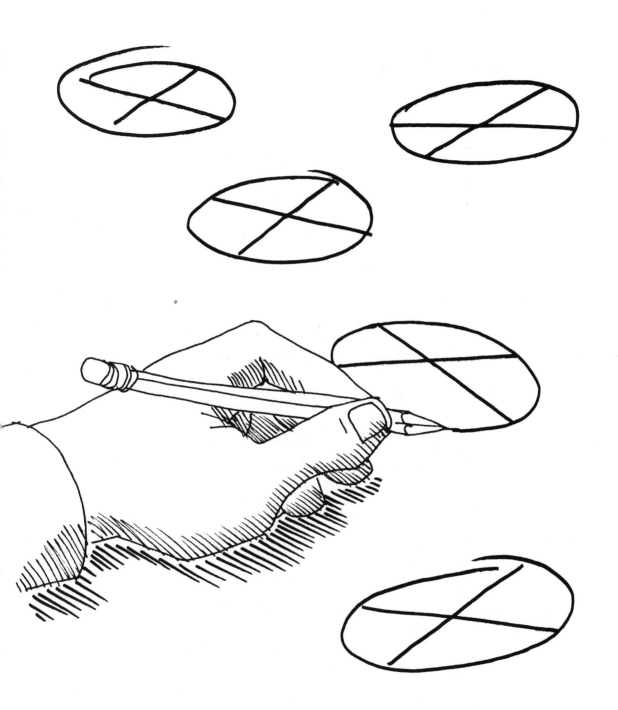

But at least one
authority takes
it beyond the
question of
which hand you
use.

Dr. Samuel Johnson,
who was probably a
closet left-hander,
seems to agree. He was
spooked by left-footedness.

To enter the
house with
the left foot
brings down
evil on the
inmates.

Psychologists are fascinated
with left-handers. They're
constantly studying
them and coming up
with reasons not to
be left-handed.

For example, recent studies by
psychologist Theodore Blau (he
of the counterclockwise circles)
show left-handers
to be . . .

stubborn,

oversensitive,

impulsive,

and embarrassing
to the family.

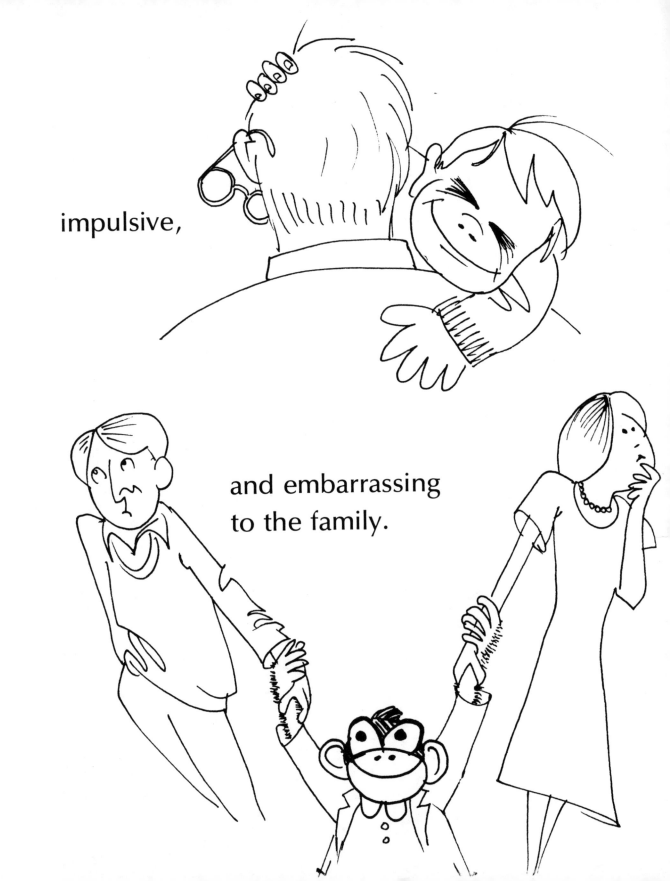

Of course, this kind of
data cuts both ways.
Left-hander Joan of Arc
was certainly impulsive, but
that's how she won battles.

And although Billy the Kid
was almost assuredly one of
those left-handers who
embarrass his family, he is
also without doubt, the
stuff of legend.

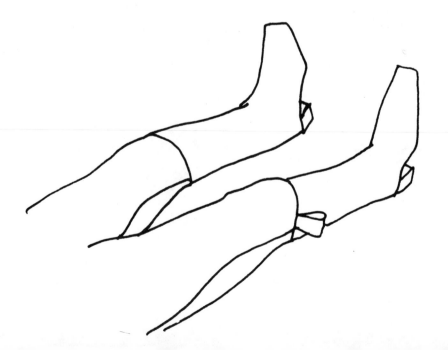

Blau goes on to find that
left-handers have difficulty
following directions.

Go pick up
your room.

And have trouble
completing projects.

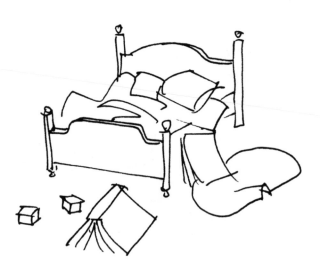

All done!

They're also likely to
have speech problems.

And to top it all off,
Blau claims that
bedwetting
among left-handers
is likely to continue
beyond the age
of three.

Another psychologist
named Blau—Abram
Blau, this time—decided
that left-handers were
just plain anti-social
and deliberately used
the "wrong" hand just
to make a mess and
raise a little hell.

This suggestion of
left-handed deviltry
harks back thousands
of years, to the time
we started throwing
salt over our left
shoulders to propitiate
the fiends who always
lurk—of course—to
the left.

Even good old
Dr. Spock, who
usually recommends
you let your kid
do almost anything,
suggests you
discourage
left-handedness in
young children.

But maybe the final, and
wisest, medical opinion
on the subject comes
from neurosurgeon Joseph
Bogan: "Right-handers
are a bunch of chocolate
soldiers. If you've seen
one, you've seen 'em all.
But left-handers are
something else again."

Well, at least everyone
agrees left-handers are special.
But are they specially good?

Or specially bad?

To find out, we must
enter a very strange world . . .
the world of the human
brain . . . a shadowy place of
surprises and contradictions,

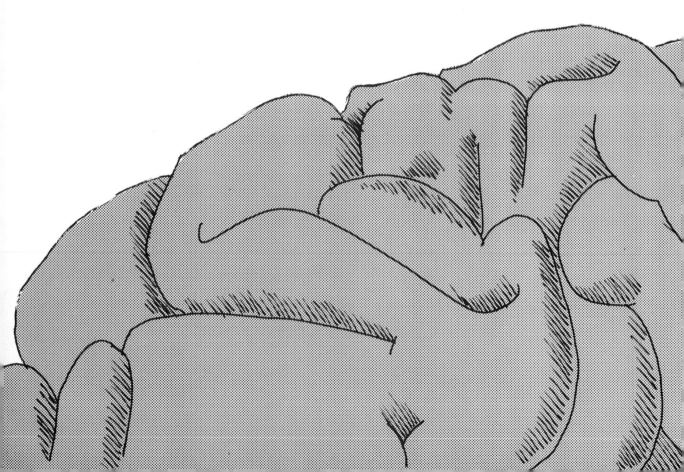

only partially mapped and
imperfectly understood.
But we know it holds the
key to the secret of
left-handedness.

The brain is made up of two
very different hemispheres. We
need both, but for different
reasons, since each has its
own functions . . .

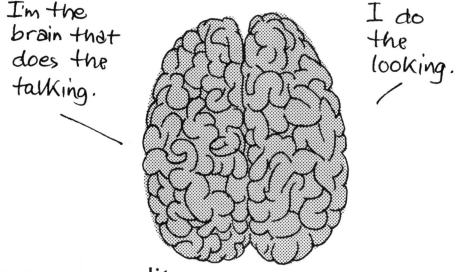

I'm the
brain that
does the
talking.

I do
the
looking.

its own personality . . .

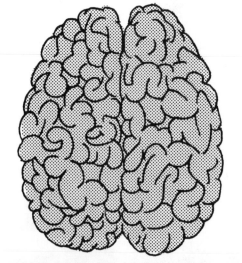

I think
and plan
and
deduce.

I groove,
baby.

its own specialties . . .

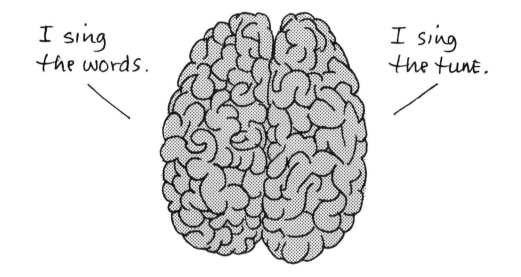

I sing the words.

I sing the tune.

and most significantly, in reference to the subject under consideration, its own hand.

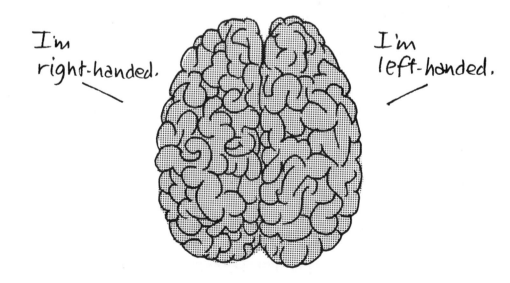

I'm right-handed.

I'm left-handed.

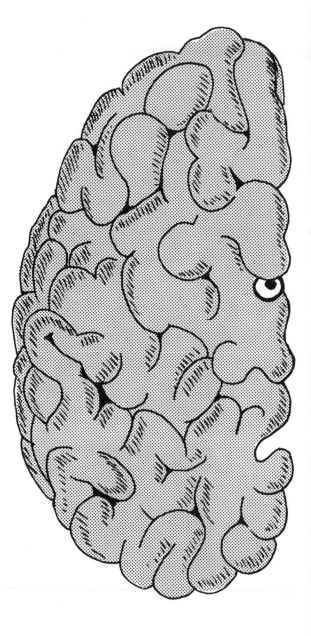

Hey! I'm in
Charge here!
It stands
to reason!
I'm the
responsible
one!

Because they have such
different points of view,

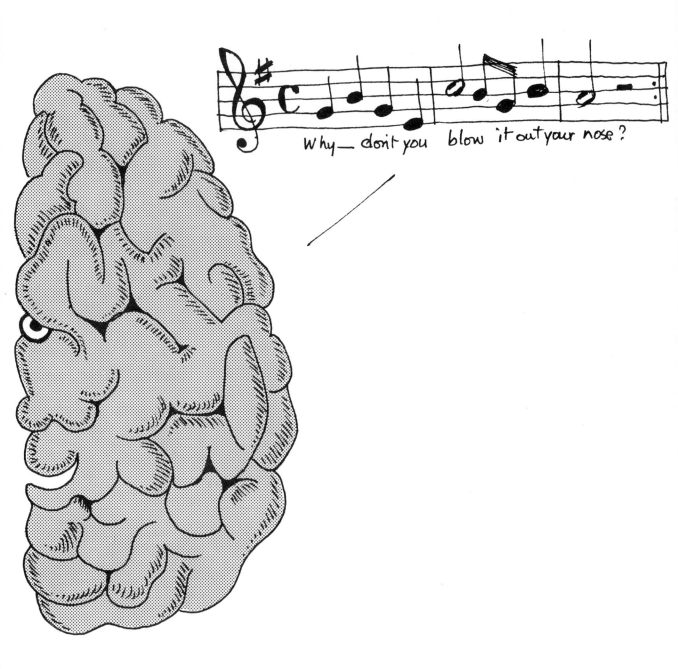

the "thinking" and "feeling" hemispheres
compete for dominance.

Generally speaking, people
with a dominant "thinking"
brain become right-handed.

It seems
only
reasonable!

While those with a
dominant "feeling" brain
become left-handed.

You might expect a
right-hander to be verbal,
analytical, and good at math.

And a left-hander to be
intuitive, and mystical, with
a strong visual sense.

Which is exactly the case.

In politics, maybe this is
why cold, heartless conservatives
are called right-wingers.

And why dreamy, bleeding heart liberals are called left-wingers.

A lot of hard
evidence shows that
most left-handers—
because they are
dominated by a different
kind of brain—are
a distinctly different
kind of people.

They literally think
differently, even when
solving the same problem as
a right-hander.

Right-handers adapt
comfortably to
abstractions.

But left-handers tend to
translate everything
into visual imagery.

Right-handers tend to
think lineally, linking
their ideas in logical order.

And therefore,
m'lord,
whereas the
party of the
first part...

Left-handers are more apt
to think holistically, skipping
over the details.

Which explains why so many creative people have been left-handed.

And why left-handers seem almost to dominate show business.

Greta Garbo

Glen Campbell

Charlie Chaplin

Marcel Marceau

Richard Pryor

George Burns

Telly Savalas

Lenny Bruce

Shirley MacLaine

Rex Harrison

Michael Landon

Jim Henson

Robert De Niro

Marilyn Monroe

And perhaps most
interesting of all, it
helps explain one of
the more intriguing
statistics of the space age.
When NASA
went searching for the
kind of imaginative,
super-reliable, multitalented
people they would
need to explore
the moon . . .

. . . one out of every four
Apollo astronauts turned
out to be left-handed—
a figure

greater than statistical
probability.

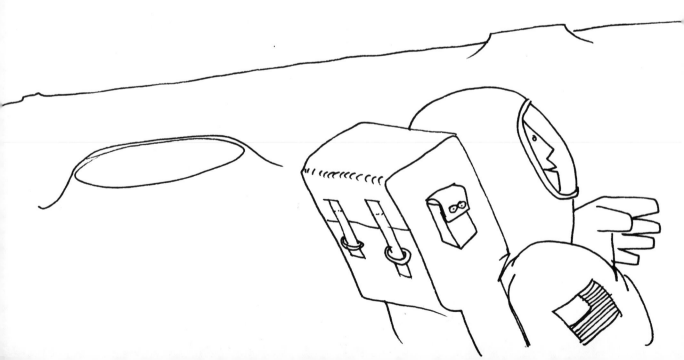

Far from being society's misfits, data like this suggests that left-handers are almost a different species. Who knows? Maybe they're the next step up in evolution.

In any case, we now know why left-handers have always believed they were special.

In their hearts, they know
they're right.